BALI
TRAVEL GUIDE

First published in 2016
by Murray Books
and Herron Book Distributors
www.herronandmurray.com

Copyright © 2016 Herron and Murray

ISBN 978-1-925449-03-7

Designed by Murray Books

Images: Shutterstock

The author and publisher have made every effort to ensure the information contained in this book
was correct at the time of going to press and accept no responsibility for any loss, injury or inconvenience
sustained by any person or organisation using this book. Some editorial may have been used from the
Public Domain.

Distributed world-wide by

CONTENTS

BALI

Bali, the famed Island of the Gods, with its varied landscape of hills and mountains, rugged coastlines and sandy beaches, lush rice terraces and barren volcanic hillsides. Set against a picturesque backdrop that showcases a colourful, deeply spiritual and unique culture, Bali stakes a serious claim to be paradise on earth. With world-class surfing and diving, a large number of cultural, historical and archaeological attractions, and an enormous range of accommodation, Bali is one of the world's most popular island destinations and one which consistently wins travel awards. Bali has something to offer a very broad range of visitors from young back-packers right through to the super-rich.

Bali is one of more than 17,000 islands in the Indonesian archipelago and is located just over 2 kilometres (almost 1.5 miles) from the eastern tip of the island of Java and west of the island of Lombok. The island, home to about 4 million people, is approximately 144 kilometres (90 mi.) from east to west and 80 kilometres (50 mi.) north to south. The word paradise is used a lot in Bali, and not without reason. The combination of friendly, hospitable people, a magnificently visual culture infused with spirituality and (not least) spectacular beaches with great surfing and diving have made Bali Indonesia's unrivalled, number one tourist attraction. Eighty percent of international visitors to Indonesia visit Bali and Bali alone. The popularity is not without its flip side - like many places in the island's south, once paradisiacal Kuta has degenerated into a congested warren of concrete, touts and scammers extracting a living by overcharging tourists. The island's visibility has also drawn the unwanted attention of terrorists in 2002 and 2005, but Bali has managed to retain its magic. Bali is a wonderful destination with something for everyone, and though heavily travelled, it is still easy to find some peace and quiet, if you like. Avoid the south of the island if you want a more traditional and genuine Balinese experience.

Bali can get very crowded in August and September, and again at Christmas and New Year. Australians also visit during school holidays in early April, late June and late September, while domestic tourists from elsewhere in Indonesia visit during national holidays. Outside these peak seasons, Bali can be surprisingly quiet and good discounts on accommodation are often available.

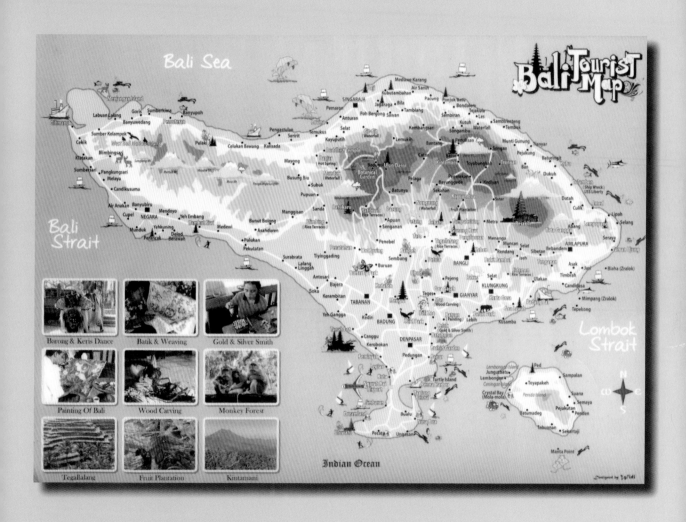

BALI'S HISTORY

The first Hindus arrived in Bali as early as 100 BC, but the unique culture that is so apparent to any current day visitor to Bali hails largely from neighbouring Java, with some influence from Bali's distant animist past. The Javanese Majapahit Empire's rule over Bali ended in the 14th century when Gajah Mada of Java defeated the Balinese king at Bedulu. The rule of the Majapahit Empire resulted in the initial influx of Javanese culture, most of all in architecture, dance, painting, sculpture and the wayang puppet theatre. All of this is still very apparent today. The very few Balinese who did not adopt this Javanese Hindu culture are known today as the Bali Aga (original Balinese) and still live in the isolated villages of Tenganan, near Candidasa and Trunyan on the remote eastern shore of Lake Batur at Kintamani.

With the rise of Islam in the Indonesian archipelago, the Majapahit Empire in Java fell, and Bali became independent near the turn of the 16th century. The Javanese aristocracy found refuge in Bali, bringing an even stronger influx of Hindu arts, literature and religion. Divided among a number of ruling rajas, occasionally fighting off invaders from now Islamic Java to the west and making forays to conquer Lombok to the east, the north of the island was finally captured by the Dutch colonialists in a series of brutal wars from 1846 to 1849. Southern Bali was not conquered until 1906, and eastern Bali did not surrender until 1908. In both 1906 and 1908, many Balinese chose death over disgrace and fought en-masse until the bitter end, often walking straight into Dutch cannons and gunfire. This manner of suicidal fighting is known as puputan. Victory was bittersweet, as the images of the puputan highly tarnished the Dutch in the international community. Perhaps to make up for this, the Dutch did not make the Balinese enter into a forced servitude, as had happened in Java, and instead tried to promote Balinese culture through their policy of Baliseering or the Balinisation of Bali. Bali became part of the newly independent Republic of Indonesia in 1945. In 1965, the military seized power in a CIA-backed coup, and state-sanctioned, anti-communist violence spread across Indonesia. In Bali, it has been said that the rivers ran red with the reprisal killings of suspected communists - most estimates of the death toll say 80,000, or about five percent of the population of Bali at the time.

The current chapter in Bali's history began in the seventies when intrepid hippies and surfers discovered Bali's beaches and waves, and tourism soon became the biggest income earner. Despite the shocks of the terrorist attacks in 2002 and 2005, the magical island continues to draw crowds, and Bali's culture remains as spectacular as ever.

See and Do
1. Tourist Information Office
2. Bali Museum
3. Catur Mukha statue
4. Palace of Satria and Royal Temples
5. Puputan Park and Bajra Sandhi
6. Pura Agung Jagatnata
7. Pura Maospahit
8. Sidik Jari Museum
9. Taman Budaya Cultural Centre

Buy
1. Ramayana
2. Matahari Duta Plaza
3. Robinsons
4. Tiara Dewata
5. Badung Central Market
6. Duta Silk
7. Gold Stores

Eat
1. Atoom Baru
2. Ayam Goreng Nyonya Suharti
3. Ayam Taliwang
4. Bali Bakery
5. Cianjur
6. Kak Man
7. Warung Nasi Bali
8. Warung Wardani
9. Kereneng Night Market

Drink
1. Kopi Bali

Sleep
1. Adi Yasa Hotel
2. Aston Denpasar
3. Genesis Hotel
4. Inna Bali Inn
5. Merta Sari Hotel
6. Nakula Familiar Hotel
7. Taman Suci Hotel
8. Tirta Lestari Hotel

Ubung

Ubung Bemo Terminal

To Tabanan

To Ubud

Gatot Subroto Permai Housing

Jl Gatot Subroto Barat

Jl Gatot Subroto

Jl Gatot Subroto

Jl Raya Buluh Indah

Jl Cokroaminoto

Jl Ahmed Yani

Jl Nangka

Jl Suli

Jl Ratna

Jl Kenyeri

Jl Nori

Jl Bisma

Jl Pattimura

Jl WR Supratman

To Sanur

2km

Jl Sutomo

Jl Setiabudi

Jl Kartini

Jl Veteren

Jl Yudistira

Jl Kepundung

Jl Melati

Jl Piawa

Jl Wibisawa

Jl Nusa Indah

Jl Katrangan

Gunung Agung Bemo Terminal

Jl Gunung Agung

Jl Arjuna

Kamboja

Kereneng Bemo Terminal

Jl Sumatera

Jl M Thamrin

Jl Gajah Mada

Jl Sulawesi

Jl Surapati

Jl Hayam Wuruk

Jl Puputan Baru

Jl Hasanudin

Jl Dewi Madri

Jl Hayam Wuruk

Jl Gunung Batukaru

Tegal Bemo Terminal

Jl Imam Bonjol

Jl PB Sudirman

Jl Diponegoro

Jl Letda Kajeng

Jl Drupadi

Jl Prof Mid Yamin

Jl Mahendrata

Jl Gunung Rinjani

Jl Letda Tantular

Jl Cokorda Agung Tresna

Jl Letda Tantular

Jl Teuku Umar

Jl Dewi Sartika

Jl Raya Puputan

1km

Jl Imam Bonjol

Sanglah Hospital

Sanglah Bemo Terminal

Renon

To Legian & Seminyak

To Legian & Kuta

N

0.5 km

0.5 Miles

Denpasar

BALI'S CULTURE

Unlike any other island in largely Muslim Indonesia, Bali has kept its unique Hindu religion and culture. Every aspect of Balinese life is suffused with religion, but the most visible signs are the tiny offerings (canang sari, or sesajen) found in every Balinese house, workplace, restaurant, souvenir stall and airport check-in desk. These leaf trays are made daily and can contain an enormous range of offering items - flowers, glutinous rice, cookies, salt, and even cigarettes and coffee! They are set out with burning incense sticks and sprinkled with holy water no less than three times a day, before every meal. Don't worry if you step on one, as they are placed on the ground for this very purpose and will be swept away anyway (But you better not step on one on purpose, because the Balinese believe it'll give you bad luck!).

Balinese Hinduism diverged from the mainstream well over 500 years ago and is quite radically different from what you would see in India. The primary deity is Sanghyang Widi Wasa (Acintya), the all-in-one god, of which other gods like Vishnu (Wisnu) and Shiva (Civa) are merely manifestations. Instead of being shown directly, Acintya is depicted by an empty throne wrapped in the distinctive poleng - a black-and-white chessboard pattern and protected by a ceremonial tedung umbrella.

The Balinese are master sculptors, and temples and courtyards are replete with statues of gods and goddesses like Dewi Sri, the goddess of rice and fertility, as well as guardians and protective demons like toothy Rakasa, armed with a club. These days, though, entire villages like Batubulan have twigged onto the tourist potential and churn out everything imaginable from Buddhas to couples entwined in acrobatic poses for the export market. Balinese dance and music are also justly famous and a major attraction for visitors to the island. As on neighbouring Java, the gamelan orchestra and wayang kulit shadow puppet theatre predominate. Dances are extremely visual and dramatic, and the most famous include:

Barong or lion dance
A ritual dance depicting the fight between good and evil, with performers wearing fearsome lion-like masks. This dance is often staged specifically for tourists as it is one of the most visually spectacular and the storyline is relatively easy to follow. Barong dance performances are not hard to find.

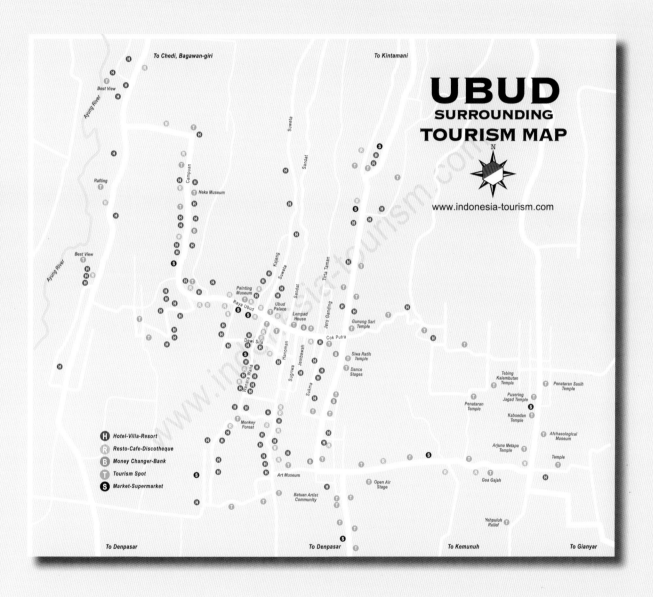

UBUD
SURROUNDING
TOURISM MAP

www.indonesia-tourism.com

To Chedi, Bagawan-giri

To Kintamani

Best View

Ayung River

Rafting

Campuan

Neka Museum

Best View

Ayung River

Suweta

Sandat

Painting Museum

Kajeng

Suweta

Sandat

Raya Ubud

Ubud Palace

Lempad House

Tirta Taman

Jero Ganding

Gunung Sari Temple

Cok Putra

Siwa Ratih Temple

Dewi Sita

Hanoman

Dance Stages

Hanoman Wina

Sugriwa

Jembawah

Sukma

Tebing Kalembutan Temple

Penataran Sasih Temple

Pusering Jagad Temple

Penataran Temple

Kaboedan Temple

Archaeological Museum

Arjuna Metapa Temple

Temple

Monkey Forest

H Hotel-Villa-Resort
R Resto-Cafe-Discotheque
B Money Changer-Bank
T Tourism Spot
S Market-Supermarket

Goa Gajah

Art Museum

Open Air Stage

Batuan Artist Community

Yehpuluh Relief

To Denpasar

To Denpasar

To Kemunuh

To Gianyar

Calonarang

A spectacular dance which is a tale of combating dark magic and exorcising the evil spirits aligned with the witch-queen Rangda. The story has many variations and rarely are two calonarang plays the same. If you can find an authentic Calonarang performance, then you are in for a truly magical experience.

Kecak or monkey dance

The Kecak was actually invented in the 1930s by resident German artist Walter Spies for a movie but a spectacle nonetheless, with up to 250 dancers in concentric circles chanting kecak kecak, while a performer in the centre acts out a spiritual dance. An especially popular Kecak dance performance is staged daily at Uluwatu Temple.

Legong Keraton

This is perhaps the most famous and feted of all Balinese dances. Performed by young girls, this is a dance of divine nymphs hailing from 12th century Java. Try to find an authentic Legong Keraton with a full-length performance. The short dance performances often found in tourist restaurants and hotels are usually extracts from the Legong Keraton.

Art, both traditional and modern, is everywhere in Bali and impossible to miss. Ubud is the artistic capital of the island with several museums and a variety of informal workshops and retail outlets. Ubud's museums showcase the works of local artists, both living and dead, as well as works by many foreign artists, who either have a strong affinity to Bali or have made the island their permanent home.

Balinese dancing has a rich history of spiritual emphasis linked to the Hindu culture. Every dance and its movements holds significance, and each tells an ancient story.

The gentleness and grace of an entire culture is personified by its traditional dancers and their exquisitely crafted costumes.

13

The fan features heavily in the traditional dances of many Asian cultures. The Kecak and Fan Dance is especially popular in Balinese dancing.

The symbiosis of water and culture are important to the Balinese, and many sacred images feature in unexpected but delightful places. Here, the sacred waters of the Tirtha Empul Temple await the faithful to arrive and bathe in them.

17

Long before the advent of Islam or Christianity in the region, the Javanese Majapahit Empire left its cultural stamp on the people and the islands of Bali.

21

Long before Balinese children learn to walk, they are taught to dance with their hands. The expressive, graceful movements of Bali's dancers seem part of the greater landscape at times.

There is a great richness of dance forms and styles in Bali; and particularly notable are those ritualistic dance dramas which involve Rangda, the witch, and the great beast Barong.

FESTIVALS AND HOLIDAYS

There are an estimated 20,000 temples (pura) on the island, each of which holds festivals (odalan) at least twice yearly. With many other auspicious days throughout the year there are always festivities going on. The large island-wide festivals are determined by two local calendars. The 210 day wuku or Pawukon calendar is completely out of sync with the western calendar, meaning that it rotates wildly throughout the year. The lunar saka (caka) calendar roughly follows the western year.

Funerals (pitra yadnya) are another occasion of pomp and ceremony, when the deceased (often several at a time) are ritually cremated in extravagantly colorful rituals (ngaben).

Galungan is a 10 day festival which comes around every 210 days and celebrates the death of the tyrant Mayadenawa. Gods and ancestors visit earth and are greeted with gift-laden bamboo poles called penjor lining the streets. The last day of the festival is known as Kuningan.

Nyepi, or the Hindu New Year, also known as the day of absolute silence, is usually in March or April. If you are in Bali in the days preceding Nyepi, you will see amazing colorful giants (ogoh ogoh) being created by every banjar. On the eve of Nyepi, the ogoh ogoh are paraded through the streets, an amazing sight which is not to be missed. There are good reasons to avoid Nyepi as well, but for many visitors, these will be outweighed by the privilege of experiencing such a unique festival. On Nyepi, absolutely everything on the island is shut down between 6AM on the day of the new year and 6AM the following morning. Tourists are confined to their hotels and asked to be as quiet as possible for the day. After dark, light must be kept to a bare minimum, and no one is allowed onto the beaches or streets. The only exceptions granted are for real emergency cases. The airport remains closed for the entire day, which means no flights into or out of Bali for 24 hours. Ferry harbours are closed as well. As the precise date of Nyepi changes every year, and isn't finally set until later in the year before, airlines will alter their bookings accordingly. This may mean that you have to alter your accommodation bookings if your flight has been brought forward or back to cater for Nyepi day.

All national public holidays in Indonesia apply in Bali, although Ramadan is naturally a much smaller event here than in the country's Muslim regions.

BALI'S CLIMATE

Daytime temperatures are pleasant, varying between 20-33º C year-round. From December to March, the western monsoon can bring heavy showers and high humidity, but days are still often sunny with the rains starting in the late afternoon or evening and passing quickly. From June to September, the humidity is low and it can be quite cool in the evenings. At this time of the year there is hardly any rain in the lowland coastal areas.

But be aware of flood along the beach from Tuban to Melasti (Kuta) because the drainage is not sufficient anymore in line with the development of occupying the land. The flood is not come in every year, but please don't stay in the ground floor, because the one to two hours flood can reach your knee on the road in front of your hotel. Even when it is raining across most of Bali, you can often enjoy sunny, dry days on the Bukit Peninsula, which receives far less rain than any other part of the island. On the other hand, in central Bali and in the mountains, you should not be surprised by cloudy skies and showers at any time of the year.

At higher elevations such as Bedugul or Kintamani, it gets distinctly chilly and you will need either a sweater or jacket after the sun sets.

A visit to Bali is not complete until you take to the water and do some island-hopping. Alone or in a group, there is no better way to get around.

The promise held in the enormous swells off of Bali's coastline attracts surfers from all over the world.

Water not only features in the cultural and spiritual life of the Balinese - playtime is equally important to the island's children.

THE REGIONS OF BALI

SOUTH BALI

The most visited part of the island by far, with Kuta Beach and chic Seminyak standout destinations. Includes Kuta, Bukit Peninsula, Canggu, Denpasar, Jimbaran, Legian, Nusa Dua, Sanur, Seminyak and Tanah Lot.

CENTRAL BALI

The cultural heart of Bali and the central mountain range. Includes Ubud, Bedugul, and Tabanan.

WEST BALI

Ferries to Java and the West Bali National Park feature, as do Negara, Gilimanuk, Medewi Beach, Pemuteran and West Bali National Park.

NORTH BALI

Quiet black sand beaches and the old capital city - includes Lovina and Singaraja.

EAST BALI

Filled with laid back coastal villages, an active volcano and the mighty Mount Agung. Includes Amed, Besakih, Candidasa, Kintamani, Klungkung, Mount Agung, Padang Bai and Tirta Gangga.

SOUTH-EASTERN ISLANDS

There are Quiet offshore islands in the southeast, popular for diving activities. Includes Nusa Lembongan, Nusa Penida and Nusa Ceningan.

Peace and serenity exude from the stonework, thatch and water of Pura Ulun Danu Temple on Lake Bratan.

Bali's sacred statuary stands sentinel over every aspect of the island's spiritual and social life.

BALI'S CITIES AND TOWNS

DENPASAR

A bustling city, the administrative centre and transport hub of the island but not a major tourist destination.

CANDIDASA

A quiet coastal town, the Bali Aga and gateway to the east coast .

KUTA

Surfer central, by far the most heavily developed area in Bali. Lots of shopping and night-life and the centre of lower-end party culture on Bali.

JIMBARAN

Sea-side resorts, a nice sheltered beach and seafood restaurants south of Kuta.

LEGIAN

Located between Kuta and Seminyak; also the name of Kuta´s main street.

LOVINA

Beautiful black volcanic sand beaches and coral reefs.

PADANG BAI

A relaxed traditional fishing village with some touristic options. A great place to enjoy the beach, snorkelling, diving and eating fish.

SANUR

Sea-side resorts and beaches popular with older families

SEMINYAK

Quieter, more upscale beachside resorts and villas just to the north of Legian, with some fashionable upscale restaurants and trendy designer bars and dance clubs.

UBUD

The centre of art and dance in the foothills, with several museums, the monkey forest and lots of arts and crafts shops

The only difficulty with a beachside bean-bag chair is when it comes to getting up - it's a hug from a best friend, an embrace of the most comforting type, or a bed in paradise.

The aquamarine perfection of Bali's tropical waters are both relaxing and inspiring - even in winter, the invitation to swim is impossible to resist.

The world revolves around food when visiting Bali, which is little wonder with the incredible taste sensations on offer.

You know you're in Bali when the umbrellas look this good - just wonderful!

Views of hidden coves, exotic resorts, natural wonders and spectacular scenery abound in Bali - the hardest part can be tearing yourself away from such sights to head down and enjoy it.

OTHER GREAT DESTINATIONS IN BALI

AMED

An area of peaceful, traditional fishing villages featuring black sand beaches, coral reefs and excellent freediving or scubadiving

BEDUGUL

Nice lakes in the mountains, a golf course, the botanical gardens and the famous Ulun Danu Bratan Temple.

BUKIT PENINSULA

The southernmost tip of Bali, with world class surfing, great beaches, and the can't-miss cliff-hanging Uluwatu Temple.

KINTAMANI

Active volcano Mount Batur, great mountain scenery, cooler temperatures and fruit growing.

MOUNT AGUNG

The highest mountain in Bali and the mother temple of Besakih.

NUSA DUA

An enclave of high-end resorts and a long, golden sand beach.

NUSA LEMBONGAN

Good diving, snorkelling and surfing and a great place to relax.

NUSA PENIDA

Wild, rugged and untamed and as off-the-beaten-path as you will get in Bali.

WEST BALI NATIONAL PARK

Trekking, bird watching and diving in Bali's only substantial natural protected area

Ubud's Elephant Camp is legendary, and its gentle giants add to the exotic experience of seeing tropical Asia at its very best.

Only the modern furniture detracts from a scene that hasn't changed for centuries. The rice fields were sculpted into terraces long before the first Europeans arrived.

Heaven on earth can be found - the search begins along Bali's stunning coastline.

The Balinese landscape often speaks of an ancient, spiritual past shrouded in mystery.

Delightful hideaways lurk around every coastal corner, leaving those who wander in to think they are the first to step foot on pristine beaches.

Sunsets and sunrises are always more spectacular near the equator. Within moments, it will be dark, but for now, nature's palette is at its most spectacular.

Flat, sandy beaches offer rolling waves and pristine waters - an escape that could be anywhere in the Caribbean or the South Pacific.

GETTING THERE AND STAYING

VISAS

All passports must be valid for a minimum of 6 months from the date of entry into Indonesia and have at least 2 blank pages available for stamps.

There are three ways of entering Indonesia:

Visa waiver. Show your passport, get stamped, that's it. Most visitors fall in this category.

Visa on arrival. Pay on arrival, get a visa in your passport, get it stamped.

Visa in advance. Obtain a visa at an Indonesian embassy before arrival.

Visitors arriving in Bali by air from a point of origin outside Indonesia will be clearing customs and immigration at Bali's Ngurah Rai International Airport may require the purchase of a visa on arrival (VOA). As of January 2014, the only type of visa on arrival available is US$35.00 for 30 days. This may be extended later at the local Immigration office for a further once only period of up to 30 days. (The previous 7 day visa on arrival is no longer available). Exact change in dollars is recommended, although a selection of other major currencies including rupiah are accepted (usually displayed at the VOA counter), and any change will usually be given in rupiah. Credit cards are accepted in Bali (but don't count on the service working).

Arriving passengers are passed through VOA (visa on arrival) issuance if applicable, then subsequently processed through immigration clearance channels for VOA, Non VOA (if the visa has been obtained prior to the time of departure), Visa waiver (for eligible nationalities) and a separate channel for Indonesian passport holders. Baggage retrieval is followed by customs and quarantine examinations including baggage X-ray checkpoints. The VOA and immigration clearance lines are integrated into several continuous lines; unlike the previous route where a passenger needed to line up at a VOA line and then to an immigration line. Tourism visit visas can be issued in advance at some Indonesian embassies prior to departure. Check well in advance of your proposed departure date at the Indonesian embassy or consulate in your home country.

Initial one month tourist visas can be extended by a further one month. There are many visa / travel agencies that can do this for you and it takes about a week or 5 working days. Costs vary but surprisingly they seem more expensive in south Bali than it is in more rural locations further away from the immigration passport office. In south Bali expect to pay between Rp 600,000 to 750,000 or even more. Elsewhere it can be as low as Rp 500,000 such as in Amed. A good place to find cheaper visa agents is at scuba diving centres. They often have divers wishing to stay longer and therefore know where to get visa extensions done cheaply for their customers.

It seems that one month visa extensions can be repeatedly applied for up to a maximum of a 6 month stay.

Consulates

Some countries have set up consulates in Bali and these are their contact details, the nation's capital Jakarta has a number of embassies representing a wide range of nationalities. The details for the Australian Embassy are:

Jalan Tantular, No. 32, Renon, Denpasar
Phone - (+62) 361 241118
Skype - (+62) 361 241118
Email - bali.congen@dfat.gov.au

For emergency contact:
Phone - (+62) 361 241118
Skype - (+62) 361 241118. Follow the instructions (press 4, wait for the information recording to begin and then press (6), this will connect you to the 24 hour Consular Emergency Centre in Canberra.

Mysteries of past worship and present interpretation fascinate both the Balinese and their visitors.

FLYING TO BALI

Most visitors will arrive at Ngurah Rai International Airport (IATA: DPS), also known as Denpasar International Airport. Despite this misleading name, the airport is actually located in Tuban between Kuta and Jimbaran, roughly 30 mins away from Denpasar. Ngurah Rai is Indonesia's third busiest international airport (after Jakarta and Surabaya) and a major hub well-connected to Australia, South-East Asia, and the rest of Indonesia.

AirAsia LCC from Kuala Lumpur (operated by (AK) AirAsia Malaysia and (QZ) Indonesia AIrAsia), Singapore, Perth, Darwin (operated by (QZ) Indonesia AIrAsia), Bangkok (operated by (FD) Thai AIrAsia)

Cathay Pacific from Hong Kong

Cebu Pacific Air LCC from Manila

China Airlines (code share Garuda Airlines) from Taipei

Eva Air from Taipei-Taoyuan

Emirates from Dubai - United Arab Emirates

Garuda Indonesia, The major national carrier serving Indonesia from Hong Kong, Kuala Lumpur, Melbourne, Nagoya-Centair, Osaka-Kansai, Perth, Seoul-Incheon

Hong Kong Express Airways from Hong Kong

Jetstar LCC from Australia - Brisbane, Darwin, Melbourne, Perth, Sydney, New Zealand

Jetstar Asia LCC (code share Qantas Airlines, operated by Valuair) from Singapore

KLM from Amsterdam (via Singapore may be operated by Singapore Airlines or Garuda on the SIN-DPS sector, Amsterdam via Kuala Lumpur (via Kuala Lumpur may be operated by Malaysian Airlines on the KUL-DPS sector)

Korean Airlines (code share Garuda Airlines) from Seoul (Incheon)

Malaysia Airlines (code share Garuda Airlines, KLM) from Kuala Lumpur

Merpati Nusantara Airlines LCC from Dili

Philippine Airlines from Manila

Qantas Airlines (operated by Jetstar, Jetstar Asia and Valuair) from Singapore, Australia, New Zealand

Qatar Airways from Doha and Singapore

Shanghai Airlines from Shanghai

Singapore Airlines from Singapore

SkyWest from Port Hedland Australia

Strategic Airlines from Australia- Brisbane, Perth, Port Hedland, Townsville

Thai AirAsia from Bangkok - Don Mueang International Airport

Thai Airways International from Bangkok-Suvarnabhumi

Transaero from Moscow-Domodedovo

Valuair LCC (operated by Jetstar Asia) from Singapore

Uni Air (charter flights) from Kaohsiung

Virgin Australia from Australia - Adelaide, Brisbane, Melbourne, Perth, Sydney

Ngurah Rai International Airport has recently been largely revamped to compensate for the growing amount of visitors to the island. A new international terminal was opened in 2013, and domestic service transferred to the old international terminal. It now features fairly modern decor, much improved signage and is generally up to par with Indonesia's other international airports. The domestic terminal's arrival area has all checkin counters on the first floor (before any security checks, unlike Jakarta's airport), with Garuda Indonesia on the left and other airlines on the right. After a single security check, which serves as the limit for non-passengers, escalators lead to a short section of shops on the second floor before opening up to the main departure area.

Restaurants and cafes are also spread out here, with lounges near the ends. There is generally ample space, even during busy hours, especially in the restaurants.

ATMs which accept Cirrus and Plus cards for withdrawals are available in airport departure and arrival areas and a range money changing kiosks including some operated by Indonesian banks such as BNI, BCA and Mandiri are available at the airport. Most ATMs for international arriving passengers are available right after exiting customs. Tourist information, along with car rentals and other services are lined up along the exiting hallway upon arrival in both terminals.

Security protocols including passenger and baggage screening are similar to other large international airports in the region. Limitations similar to those in the EU and US are placed upon the carrying of fluids and other so- called security items in hand luggage. International passengers should be prepared for scrutiny of their baggage, including all carry-on items. When departing, you will likely pass through a total of three security checkpoints, and possibly a further one at the boarding gate, so be patient, particularly when things are busy. The staff do not generally require the removal of belts, laptops and jackets like other large airports - signage may indicate this, but they are not always enforced. Belts that set off the metal detector will need to be sent through, however. Security protocols at the domestic terminal are similar to those applied at other Indonesian domestic hub airports, with baggage and carry-on screening, x-ray, metal detection, hand inspections and other security measures in place for departing passengers. Porters now usually will not take control of your luggage unless they either ask you, or you ask them for their assistance (depending on which one comes first). If you do utilise them; tipping is based on size of your baggage and the time spent helping you get through customs. In most cases, your baggage will be off of the conveyor belt and lined up on the side by the time you make your way to the baggage claim area.

When departing Bali, you are subject to the airport departure tax which should be included in the ticket price. If your ticket was purchased before Feb 9th 2015 then your airline may advise you to pay online or via the PSC payment counters that are still available at the airport. The fee for international flight is Rp. 200.000. Departing Bali to overseas destinations has also largely improved after some high profile cases regarding corrupt officials. Be aware of items that require declaration and make sure they are appropriately reported. Baggage does not need to be wrapped to be checked in - the wrapping stalls are more of an optional measure. The adjacent island of Lombok also has a new international airport and in the near future it is likely to be able to assist in balancing the incoming traffic load by reducing some of the onward destination traffic currently arriving in Bali. The new airport in Lombok also provides a nearby safe alternative landing site for wide-bodied aircraft in case of any emergency.

Perhaps it's the deep spiritual culture of the islands, or maybe it lies in the imagination- the sensation is unique and exhilarating and speaks of the promise to be had in a new day.

GETTING AROUND IN BALI

Bali is a fairly large island and you will need a method to get around if you plan on exploring more than the hotel pool. Rapid, seemingly uncontrolled development and an aging infrastructure, mean that the roads struggle to cope. In major tourist areas the traffic is chaotic, and there are daily jams. Particular blackspots are Ubud, Kuta, Seminyak and Denpasar. For different excursions around the island, it is common to join a tour via your hotel or at one of the many street agencies which are found everywhere in booths normally marked Tourist Information.

Once you arrive at your destination you may encounter difficult walking conditions as sidewalks in most parts of Bali are simply the covered tops of storm-water drains and in many places only 60cm (2 ft) wide. This makes for uncomfortable single-file walking next to traffic. Often sidewalks are blocked by a motorbike or a caved-in section, necessitating dangerous darting into traffic. Many of the island's conventional streets are simply not pedestrian-friendly. Beach areas and major tourist areas are easier to walk around and Sanur in particular has a wide beachfront pathway with many cafes and bars. But although the walking conditions are difficult, they are by no means impossible. Lots of tourists and locals travel the roads by foot and even the traffic is generally very accommodating to pedestrians if it is given time to react.

FLYING WITHIN BALI

A number of domestic airlines operate as LCC - low cost or budget carriers. It is a difficult distinction for some operators as they may be using a low cost model but not promoting or identifying themselves as doing this. Wings Air is a LCC of Lion Air, Citilink is a LCC of Garuda Airlines. Some are smaller regional operators REG or feeder airlines.

Citilink LCC from Jakarta

Garuda Indonesia from Jakarta, Mataram, Surabaya, Semarang, Ujung Pandang (Makassar), Yogyakarta

Indonesia Air Asia LCC from Bandung, Jakarta, Yogyakarta

IAT (Indonesia Air Transport) from Mataram, Labuan Bajo

Lion Air LCC from Jakarta, Jogyakarta (Yogyakarta), Menado, Ujung Pandang (Makassar), Surabaya

Tiger Air LCC from Jakarta

Merpati Nusantara Airlines LCC from Bandung, Bima, Ende. Jakarta, Kupang, Lauanbajo, Mataram, Maumere, Surabaya, Tambolaka, Waingapu

Pelita Air Service Charter

Sky Aviation REG from Banywangi, Labuan Bajo, Mataram

Sriwijaya Air LCC from Jakarta

Travira Air Charter from Benete/Sumbawa

Trigana REG from Mataram

Trans Nusa REG from Bima, Ende, Kupang, Labuanbajo, Mataram, Ruteng, Sumbawa, Tambolaka

Wings Air REG LCC Bima, Kupang, Labuhanbajo, Mataram, Maumere, Semarang, Surabaya, Malang, Tambolaka

From Bali's centre to its East, volcanic mountains and ranges proliferate. From those mountains, the landscape below is a picture-perfect tropical idyll.

BALI BY BOAT

Ferries cross from Ketapang on the island of Java to Gilimanuk in western Bali every 15 min, 24 hr every day. These are very cheap, and the crossing takes just 30 min (plus sometimes considerable waiting around for loading and unloading). A number of speedboats, catamarans and day cruises operate into Benoa Harbour near Kuta (~2 hr) and Padangbai (80 min) from Nusa Lembongan and the Gili Islands of Lombok. These are convenient for some travellers but are frequently priced much higher than the equivalent air crossing. Crossing times are subject to weather and other operational conditions and trip times can longer than those publicised.

Caution should be used in selecting a suitable operator and craft for a fast boat crossing to Lombok or Nusa Lembongan. Some of the operators on these routes use inappropriate equipment and have inadequate levels of crew training, personnel and safety equipment. The Lombok Strait fast boat crossing can be subject to inclement weather and equipment breakdowns. Boarding an overloaded craft or departing in adverse weather conditions may lead to serious disappointment. Currently there are no operators offering craft suitable for open water all-weather crossings. Rather they are operating light duty hulled craft of fibreglass or aluminium construction powered by outboard petrol engines. One of the current operators plans to introduce a more suitably specified and equipped craft sometime in the 1st or 2nd quarter of 2011. The new boat will be powered by diesel inboard engines and have a more robust hull construction appropriate to open water use.

A previous craft of similar specification was withdrawn from this route as operations could not be sustained in competition with the lower cost base alternatives. Two of the light duty craft have already sunk whilst carrying passengers, fortunately they had not yet entered open waters at the time, fortunately nearby assistance was available and there were no fatalities.

There are also public ferries from Lembar, Lombok, to Padang Bai every few hours, with the trip taking around 3 to 4 hours. This service has a notable safety, operational and equipment standards issues, some ferries are better than others, or worse depending upon your perspective. Delays are commonplace due to loading and unloading issues and services may be cancelled or postponed during periods of inclement weather. It may be prudent to avoid sea crossings during the monsoonal period when sea conditions may lead to deteriorated comfort levels or a dangerous crossing.

See the Nusa Lembongan, Gili Islands and Lombok articles for full details concerning travelling and arriving in Lembongan, Lombok and it's nearby islands. Cruise ships occasionally stop so that passengers can tour or shop. Some ships still anchor off-shore toward the southeast side of the island and tender guests to shore. Modest-sized ships can choose to dock at the port of Benoa not far from Denpasar, Kuta and Sanur. The dock area is basically industrial, with few amenities and no ATMs, but masses of taxis are usually ready to whisk you to nearby destinations at a moderate cost.

Surrounded by water and high, volcanic mountains in places, Bali offers peace, serenity and a sense of being removed from everything but the soothing calm of nature.

BALI BY BUS

The Perama Bus Company serves the budget traveller well in Bali and beyond, and they have offices in several major tourist destinations on the island. There are other scheduled shuttle buses between many of Bali's most popular destinations, and these are cheap and reliable. Check locally advertised services (you cannot miss them) and book one day in advance. A new Trans Sarbagita government bus service operates on Bali since August 2011. The buses are comfortable, air-conditioned (similar to Transjakarta Busway but even more spacious), and the fare is only Rp 3,500. These buses stop only at permanent elevated bus stops built on the road curb. As of June 2012, only Route 2 was operating (Route 1 and Route 3 are planned to be open soon).

The buses serving Route 2 start from Batubulan bemo terminal, go via Jalan Bypass Ngurah Rai (stopping in Sanur on the way) and Dewa Ruci statue (Kuta roundabout, also known as Simpang Siur roundabout) to Central Parkir Kuta (near Giant supermarket on Jalan Raya Kuta, a kilometer or so inland from the main tourist areas of Kuta), make a loop via Sunset Road back to Kuta roundabout, and go south all the way to Nusa Dua, then go back. For visitors, the main advantage is there's no need now to change bemos and to deal with 2-3 bemo drivers to get to Batubulan terminal (from where direct bemos to Ubud, Kintamani and other north and north-eastern destinations are available) or to Sanur. Those going to Nusa Dua or Benoa may find the southern part of the route useful. The bus stop nearest to the airport is Central Parkir Kuta, a Blue Bird taxi caught outside of the airport gate will cost you around Rp 25,000. If boarding at Central Parkir Kuta, beware that both southbound (Nusa Dua) and northbound (Batubulan) buses seem to use the same stop - if there are no signs on the bus, ask the conductor or other people waiting for the bus.

There are direct bus services to Bali from all major cities on Java and Lombok that link with ferries for sea crossings. These are cheap and easy, but slow.

Tip : Trans SARBAGITA bus company (https://www.facebook.com/pages/Trans-SARBAGITA/114451925323386) operates a fully air conditioned buses all coloured in blue. One way adult fare to any destination on the bus route will only cost you Rp3,500 per person. If you want to take the bus, exit left and continue walking until you are outside of the airport building (about 200 metres) until you reach a roundabout. Wait at the opposite end of the roundabout. If you are not sure, ask around. Tell the bus driver that you want to go to Central Parkir Kuta. You can continue your journey to your hotel in nearby Kuta or Legian by taking a cab at a much lower fare.

Bemos are minivans which serve as a flexible bus service (also known as Shuttle Bus) and are Bali's traditional form of transportation. However they have largely given way to metered taxis in the south. Fares on shared bemos can be very cheap, but drivers will often insist that foreign tourists charter the entire vehicle, in which case they will usually ask for a price equivalent to a taxi or even more.

Once you accustom yourself to the island traffic, a scooter tour around Bali is one of the best ways to see the sights.

TAXIS IN BALI

Metered taxis are very common in southern Bali as far north as Denpasar but few and far between elsewhere. The starting flagfall charge is Rp 5,000 for the first two kilometres and the meter ticks up Rp 5,000 per km after that. Waiting time is charged at Rp 30,000 per hour. Trips outside southern Bali will incur an extra charge of 30%, as the driver has to go back empty.

By far the largest and most reliable taxi company is Bali Taksi/Blue Bird. They have a telephone call service (+62) 361 701111 for both instant taxis and for advance bookings. If you are hailing a taxi on the street, Bali Taksi cars are sky blue with a white top light. The cars are modern and the drivers well-informed with a decent level of English-language ability. There are several other reliable taxi companies but these are not always easy to identify. If entering a taxi with no working meter, you can negotiate a price if you know how to bargain. Alternatively, always insist on the meter being turned on, and leave the taxi if that request is not met. Due to the traffic, the taxis may refuse to use the meter in traffic jams, and you need to negotiate a price. Expect to pay around Rp 5,000 to travel from Kuta to Legian.

If day-tripping, it is often cheaper and more convenient to arrange for your taxi to wait and take you back.

In terms of transportation from the airport, Ngurah Rai is not too bad, but is also far from being perfect. Some hotels organise free transfers from the airport, but plenty of public taxis are also available: go to the ticketing booth. Just after you x-ray your bag, you'll enter a concourse. You can go left or right and all the waiting hotel drivers will on the other side of a wall from you. Head left and the (tiny) ticketing booth will be on your right, just before the air-conditioned duty free area. Here you can buy a fixed-fare ticket and a driver will be assigned to you trouble-free. However, the ticketing booth closes after the last flight arrival for the day and re-opens at 8 am, so anyone wanting an airport taxi during this period should be prepared to haggle or seek the alternatives described below. Beware being overcharged by the staff behind the counter, citing reasons such as new rates. This commonly happens to travelers who appear new to Bali and unsure of the pricing, and can be as much as 100% more. It is best to determine your destination's locality and prepare the exact amount for a trip to that area. At the counter, hand that amount over while confidently stating your destination. If necessary, mention the pricing on the board behind the counter to reinforce the amount you give. Note that the price is per car, not per person. If you are travelling on a restricted budget, you can flag down a Blue Bird Taxi from outside the airport gate (3-5 minutes walk from both terminals). Blue Bird Taxis are safe and reliable, and their metered fares are somewhat cheaper than the prepaid taxi fares. Depending on how much baggage you have and how bulky it is, you might want to evaluate whether all that extra effort is worth it to save a few dollars. Metered ride to Kuta, for example, would generally cost Rp 20,000 to 30,000.

If you do make the effort to walk outside the airport to the street, you can also flag down a bemo (local minivan). Most of the bemos in this area will be heading to Kuta (road to Kuta heads to the left if looking out from the airport gate), but don't absolutely bank on it, and be prepared for a hot, crowded journey. It should cost

no more than a few thousand rupiah per person (ask the driver beforehand). There's also an air conditioned bus service called Trans Sarbagita that runs following route Term. Batu Bulan (Gianyar) - Tohpati (DPS) - Sanur (DPS) - Kuta Central Park (Badung) - Jimbaran (Badung) - Nusa Dua (Badung), occasionally the bus heading to and from Nusa Dua will stop at the airport. There is no marked Trans Sarbagita bus stop at the airport. Bus stops at the roundabout at the left side from the airport exit. The bus fare is 3.500 RP for adults and 2.500 for students.

Prepaid Taxi Fares from Ngurah Rai Airport to Main Bali Destinations

(These are a guide and subject to change)

Kuta Rp	50,000
Tuban Rp	35,000
Legian Rp	55,000
Seminyak Rp	60,000 to 70,000
Jimbaran Rp	70,000 to 80,000
Denpasar Rp	70,000 to 100,000
Sanur Rp	90,000
Nusa Dua Rp	95,000 to 110,000
Ubud Rp	105,000 to Rp 250,000
Padang Bai Rp	365,000
Candidasa Rp	385,000
Amed Rp	400,000
Lovina Rp	400,000 to 450,000

DRIVING IN BALI

Driving in Bali is on the left-hand side. Car and motorbike rentals are widely available but you should think very carefully about your ability to handle driving in Bali with its lack of formal traffic rules. Consider hiring a car and driver as you can relax, be safe and not get lost. If you rent a car to drive yourself, a modern four door Toyota Avanza or Daihatsu Xenia should cost Rp 200,000-250,000 per day. If on a tighter budget, you should be able to get an old, rough Suzuki Jimny from about Rp 90,000 to 110,000 per day.

Rental car services owned by individuals or companies are easy to find in Bali and this is the best option for first time visitors. Using a rental car with a driver is certainly cheaper than taxis and far more efficient than using other public transportation. The drivers are usually English-speaking and they can also act as informal tourist guides recommending good destinations and restaurants. Choosing to rent from a large car company is naturally more expensive than sourcing from a private individual. Ask hotel staff to recommend a good individually owned rental car with a knowledgeable driver.

Price varies between Rp 300,000 to 600,000 per day (usually defined as 10 hr) depending on your negotiation skills and the class/age of the car. Make sure the price includes petrol and driver for the day. Petrol costs, after the removal of some government subsidies in recent years, have escalated dramatically (although still very cheap by international standards) and the distance travelled is a factor if you have not fixed a daily price. The day price usually includes any parking fees. There are differing views on whether to offer to buy lunch for your driver. For those on a tight schedule, visiting most of the major tourist destinations in Bali will need about 3 days with a rental car and driver. Commonly driver could accompany you to the tourist destinations in Bali. The places are not well recognized by the public or written down by tourism guiding book.

WALKING STREET

PASSION OF COLOURFUL PARADISE

Luxury Condominium at Pratumnak Hill   ointpatta

416 4

MOTOR CYCLING IN BALI

Renting motorcycles or scooters can be a frightening yet fascinating experience. They are typically 125cc, some with automatic transmissions, and rent for between Rp 40,000 and 100,000 per day (for a week or more, cheaper price can be bargained). In areas outside of the tourist enclaves of south Bali, a motorbike is a wonderful way to see the island, but in south Bali, with its crush of traffic, the chances of an accident are greatly increased. Bali is no place to learn to ride a motorbike.

Riding a motorbike without a helmet is illegal throughout Indonesia and that requirement is frequently enforced by the local police in Bali. Reasonably priced helmets can be purchased in Denpasar but a renter should supply a suitable helmet/s with the motorbike. The road traffic regulations were amended in 2009 to require the illumination of head lamp and rear lamp on a motorbike during daylight hours. Police in Bali have initiated a long running information campaign to road users informing them of the requirement. Signs have been placed upon roadways advising of the regulations and the intention to enforce them. These signs are only provided in Bahasa Indonesian. This is a safety initiative and means that lights must be on at all times when riding a motorbike on any roadway in Bali. Despite the apparent disregard by local road users the use of turn signals is also required.

Driving in Bali requires an International Driving Permit (IDP), plus your own home country of residence's drivers licence Both these documents must correctly match the type and class of vehicle being driven or they are invalid. Both must be carried and are often required to be presented in roadside police stops. This requirement is actively enforced by the police throughout Bali. If riding a motorbike then a full motor bike endorsement appropriate to that class of motorbike is required on both the IDP and the home country issued drivers licence. Do not under any circumstances ride a motorbike or drive a car without a proper licence. A car licence alone is not sufficient to ride a motorbike; the licence must clearly permit you to ride a motorbike in the country of issue and the appropriate section of the IDP must be endorsed as well. Insurance is not provided by the motorbike renters so you are responsible for any damage. If you do hit a local person, either on foot, on motorcycle, or in a car, you can expect to pay a very large sum of money to make restitution. Street signs are infrequent and ambiguous. If you are not familiar with the road system and comfortable riding a motorbike at home then this may be ill advised and dangerous to learn. Thoroughly check your travel insurance policy to ensure that your cover is still in place whilst operating or riding upon a motor bike or scooter or driving a car.

CYCLING IN BALI

Travel by bicycle is quite possible and provides a very different experience than other means of transport. You should bring your own touring bike, or buy locally— there is at least one well stocked bike shop in Denpasar, but with a racing/mountain bike focus. Bicycles are also widely available for rent and some of the better hotels will even provide them free of charge. While traffic conditions may appear challenging at first, you will acclimatise after a few days, especially once you escape the chaotic heavy traffic of southern Bali.

For some, there is no better way to see Bali than from a scooter.

Bali has a beach for every taste, catering to those who love vibrancy, colour and sound as well as others seeking peace and solitude.

LANGUAGE

Balinese is linguistically very different from Bahasa Indonesia, although the latter is the lingua franca in Indonesia and is spoken by practically everyone in Bali. In tourist regions, English and some other foreign languages are widely spoken. Balinese is a difficult language, and any visitor who makes an effort to speak a few words will be especially warmly received by the local people.

BALI'S LANDSCAPE

Most of the coastline of Bali is fringed by beaches of some type, with the exceptions being some important areas of mangrove forest in the southeast, and certain parts of the Bukit Peninsula where high cliffs drop straight to the crashing waves of the Indian Ocean. Unsurprisingly, given the volcanic nature of the island, black sand is the norm, but there are also some beaches in the south which have fine-grained white sand. Beaches that are especially safe for swimming include Jimbaran Bay and virtually all of the north coast. At all times though, visitors should be aware of and obey local swimming safety markers—far too many visitors to Bali drown each year after ignoring these. Bali's popular southern beaches are sometimes not the cleanest you will find. This is particularly true during the height of the wet season (December to January), when the heavy rains cause extensive agricultural run-off and garbage to be washed onto the beaches.

Away from the coast, Bali is largely lush, green and fertile, and rice paddies are the dominant agricultural feature of the island. In some areas, paddies take the form of dramatic sculpted terraces which efficiently utilise every available acre of land for cultivation.

Especially beautiful examples of terraced paddies can be found in the centre of the island north of Ubud and in east Bali around Tirta Gangga. Elsewhere, gently rolling rice fields make for very pleasing rural scenery. All of Bali's mountains are volcanoes, some long dormant and some still active. At 3,142 metres (10,308 ft), magnificent Mount Agung dominates the landscape of East Bali and has not erupted since 1963. Much more active is Mount Batur, which permanently smolders and periodically produces a large bang and plumes of ashy smoke as pressure is released from within. Taking only two hours to climb, Batur is one of the most accessible active volcanoes in the whole of Indonesia.

BALI'S TEMPLES

Bali's best-known attractions are its countless Hindu temples. Each village is required by adat (customary law) to construct and maintain at least three temples: the pura puseh (temple of origin) located at the kaja (pure) side of the village, the pura desa (village temple) at the centre for everyday community activities and the pura dalem (temple of the dead) at the kelod (unclean) end. Wealthy villages may well have more than these three obligatory temples, and additionally all family compounds have a temple of some nature. The nine directional temples (kayangan jagat) are the largest and most prominent. These are located at strategic points across Bali and are designed to protect the island and its inhabitants from dark forces. Pura Luhur Uluwatu (Uluwatu Temple), at the southern tip of Bali, is easily accessed and hence very popular, as is Tanah Lot. For the Balinese, the "mother temple" of Besakih on the slopes of Mount Agung is the most important of all and sits above the nine. The other seven directional temples

Music and percussion play an integral role in the sound of Bali, and its traditional drummers have to be seen to be believed.

are Pura Ulun Danu Bratan, Pura Ulun Danu Batur, Pura Pasar Agung, Pura Lempuyang Luhur, Goa Lawah, Pura Masceti and Pura Luhur Batukaru. All of these are located on either rugged high ground or at the water's edge, and this is a clear indication of the likely source of dark forces as far as the Balinese are concerned.

Balinese temple design is an involved subject and one which baffles many visitors. Local geography has a fundamental effect on design, and two temples are rarely the same. Everything you see, be it decorative or structural, has a specific, well-considered function which may be of an earthly or spiritual nature. There are, though, general elements which are common to the vast majority of temples, which are always split into three courtyards: jaba (outer courtyard) , jaba tengah (middle courtyard) and jeroan (inner courtyard). Each of these courtyards contains various structures and/or shrines of differing levels of importance. The tiered, black-thatched roofs that you see on temples are made from a palm fibre, and this material is not permitted to be used for any roof other than those on temples. The elegant, pagoda-like tiered structure is itself called a meru (named after sacred Mount Meru (Mahameru), the home of the gods), and the most dramatic of them can consist of as many as 11 tiers. The number of tiers, though, is always an odd number.

The temple entrance is always on the kelod axis point (facing away from Mount Agung) of the compound and is usually a gateway of some nature. This leads into the jaba which is the domain of humans and all things earthly. The jaba contains only minor shrines, is where some celebratory dance performances take place, and during special ceremonies is where the foods stalls are set up. Non-Hindu tourists are nearly always allowed to visit this part of a temple. A gateway called a candi bentar leads into the central courtyard which is called the jaba tengah. This is the intermediary point between our earthly domain and the realm of the Gods, and this is where daily offerings are prepared in an open pavilion called a paon. The jaba tengah also usually contains a large pavilion called a wantilan, which is used for special dance performances.

The kori agung gate leads into the jeroan—the inner sacred area. This houses the most important shrines to different Hindu gods and deities and is where serious rituals and prayers take place. Shrines are many and varied but usually include a padmasana, the throne of the supreme deity Sanghyang Widi Wasa. The large pavilion in this section is called a gedong pariman, which is always left completely empty to allow the gods to visit during ceremonies. Sometimes properly dressed visitors will be allowed into the jeroan and at

Shivaite temple statuary at Pura Ulun Danu.

other times not; it depends on the individual temple and the ceremonies that have been, or are about to be, performed. The most common and practical architectural features to be found in virtually all temples are gazebo pavilions called bales. Each has a raised seating section and either an alang-alang (grass-thatched) or tali duk (black palm fibre-thatched) roof and has a myriad of social functions. Bales can serve as a place for the gamelan orchestra to sit, as a village meeting point, host dance performances or simply be a place of rest for worshipers. This part of traditional Balinese temple architecture has been copied by hotels all over the island and in the wider world. The open grass-roofed pavilions you see everywhere in Bali are all derived from this original piece of temple design.

To enter any temple you must be appropriately dressed with a sarong and sash.

These are always available for rental at the large temples which attract a lot of tourists (usually included if you're paying to enter, else a few thousand rupiah per set), but it's better to buy one of each when you arrive and use them throughout your visit.

Tirtha Empul Temple's sacred fountain heads.

The origins of Bali's earliest religion lies at the peak of Java's Borobudur Temple

MUST VISIT AND MUST DO IN BALI

Bali's Hindu culture and history is both extraordinary and unique. Many visitors get so wrapped up in shopping, partying and beach life to miss the opportunity to understand and absorb at least some of this. You cannot fail to see temples, come across ceremonies and witness daily offerings, and those who take the time and effort to understand what is going on around them will find their visit very rewarding.

There are several hot springs to be discovered in Bali. One of them, on the north coast of the island near Lovina, is Air Banjar, where stone mouth carvings allow hot water to pass between the pools, which are set in lush gardens. Another good choice is at Toya Bungkah on the shores of Lake Batur, high in the north eastern mountains.

Bali is a paradise for spa lovers, and all sorts of treatments are widely available. The Balinese lulur body scrub with herbs and spices - traditionally performed before a wedding ceremony—is particularly popular. Balinese massage is usually done with oil and involves long, Swedish-style strokes. In steep contrast to exorbitant western massage fees, Balinese massage is incredible value, and visitors should definitely avail themselves of this luxury. In local salons, a one-hour full body massage will cost between Rp 70,000 and 100,000, and the 2 hr mandi lulur, which incorporates a body scrub and hydrating yogurt body mask in addition to the massage, will cost about Rp 150,000. The curiously named creambath is a relaxing scalp and shoulder massage, usually lasting 45 min, in which a thick conditioning cream is worked through the hair and into the scalp. A cream-bath typically costs about Rp 60,000. Note that these same services in an upscale hotel will cost many times more. Fish spa, where small fish will nibble dead skin off your feet and hands, is an unusual spa treatment that is recommended for the adventurous and is available for around Rp 35,000 for 15 minutes (December 2012 prices). Bali is host to some of the finest yoga and well-being centres and retreats in the world. You can find an abundance of amazing yoga classes to suit all levels in most of the tourist areas. Look for the best yoga centres in Ubud and Seminyak. Bali is also now home to a number of renowned yoga teacher training centres.

Weddings in Bali have become very popular in recent years. Many couples who are already legally married choose Bali as the place to renew their vows. Full wedding-organising services are widely available: ceremony arrangements, photography, videography, flowers, musicians, dancers and catering. There are several wedding chapels available that are usually attached to luxury hotels, and the number is growing all the time. There are many professional organisers to handle your wedding in Bali, and these are easily found through the Internet. Destination weddings, featuring all types of religious and presentation arrangements, are becoming increasingly popular, with large private villas being one of the island's many offerings for venues.

An excellent way to get to know and understand more of the country is to do some volunteer work. There are organisations that arrange work for international volunteers in Bali and other places in the region. Volunteers can for example teach English at some non-profit organizations.

Beautiful beaches, luxury hotels, sterling service and Balinese smiles. There really isn't anything else that could make the experience better.

Getting Out And About

There are many interesting scuba diving sites around Bali. Particularly popular are the wreck of USAT Liberty at Tulamben in the east, the chilled out coral bommies in Padang Bai, the serene reefs around Menjangan Island in the northwest, and dramatic drift diving off Nusa Penida in the south. Bali is a major teaching centre, and there are numerous reputable dive centres around the island affiliated with PADI and SSI. Choose a dive centre operating their own boats on dive sites where strong currents are present in order to increase safety. For those who want their diving to make a difference as well, dive voluntourism has gain a foothold in Bali, such as in Sea Communities in Les Village, Tejakula, where divers could help rebuild coral reefs and learn to catch ornamental fish in a sustainable way. Freediving Amed and Tulamben are fast becoming recognised as the best place in Bali to learn freediving (apnea or breath-hold diving).

Warm waters, crowds of young backpackers, cheap living and reliable waves keep Bali near the top of world surfing destinations. The southern coast at Kuta, Legian and Canggu, the Bukit Peninsula and Nusa Lembongan are the primary draws. Expert surfers usually head for the big breaks off the Bukit Peninsula, whilst beginners will find the gentler, sandy areas between Kuta and Legian to be ideal for learning. All Bali's surf beaches are described in the "Indo Surf and Lingo" surfing guidebook, together with Free Bali Tide Charts on their website. There are formal surf schools on Legian beach and Kuta beach. The more adventurous might like to to try informal lessons from one of the many local self-styled surf teachers to be found hanging on any beach in South Bali. Regular surf reports are provided by Baliwaves.

The waters of Serangan harbour are protected from big waves and swells by a reef, but open to the winds. It is an excellent location for the sport of sailing. You can easily drive onto Serangan island as it is connected to Bali by a bridge. When driving to the island you will see a spectacular view of the bay on your left. Many private yachts and magnificent traditional Indonesian Phinisi schooners are moored in the smooth waters of the bay. On the beach front of Serangan you may meet other sailors who come to learn or practice their skills and share their knowledge and experience of yachting in Indonesia. There are a number of reputable white-water rafting operators in the Ubud area, and the rafting is of good quality, especially in the wet season. If you want to go in non commercial area and feel more sensations you can also do canyoning. For further info about white water rafting in Bali, you can visit Bali River Rafting.

Sport fishing is an increasingly popular activity with visitors to the island. Trolling, jigging and bottom fishing can all be very rewarding, with large game far from unusual. Charters are available from many coastal areas but the most popular points with a competitive range of options are Benoa Harbour and nearby Serangan close to Kuta, just to the north in Sanur and Padang Bai on the east coast.

Other Sports, Adventure and Family Activities

Bali has become a famous destination for golfers and there are 5 Golf Courses: Bali Handara Kosaido Country Club in the mountains near Bedugul, the Bali Golf & Country Club in Nusa Dua, a 9-hole course at the Grand Bali Beach Hotel in Sanur, the Nirwana Bali Golf Club near Tanah Lot, and the New Kuta Golf Course at Pecatu on the Bukit Peninsula.

Terraced into the landscape of Bali's mountainous regions millennia ago, even the centre of its agriculture has a languid, relaxing feel to it.

Visitors can see animals at the Bali Zoo in Singapadu near Ubud, at the Bali Bird Park, at the Taro Elephant Park, and at the Bali Marine and Safari Park located near Gianyar. Many companies also provide adventure activities such as Paragliding at Nusa Dua, Mountain Cycling in the hills of Ubud or downhill cycling from Bedugul and Kintamani, Jungle Trekking, Bungy Jumping on the beach in Seminyak, Horse Riding in Seminyak and Umalas, and Hiking in the rice fields near Ubud and many other places in the hills.

Nature can be observed while trekking in West Bali National Park, at the Butterfly Park (Taman Kupu Kupu) in Wanasari, or at the Bali Botanical Gardens in Bedugul. Inside the Botanical Gardens, visitors can also get a bird's-eye view of nature from the Bali Treetop Adventure Park.

Boat Services

Boat services run regularly to Lombok, Flores and islands further east. Combined bus and ferry services will take you to destinations in Java such as Yogyakarta.

GILI ISLANDS

The Gili Islands are three tiny islands off Lombok. A backpacker favourite fast going upmarket and easily accessed by direct boat services.

KOMODO

An island and national park in East Nusa Tenggara. The island is famous for the Komodo dragon. Accessible most easily by air via Labuan Bajo on Flores. Flight time 80-90 minutes.

LOMBOK

An unspoiled island east of Bali with beaches, waterfalls and volcanoes. Direct boat services or 20 minutes by air.

SURABAYA

Surabaya in East Java can be reached via executive bus from Ubung bus terminal for as little as 150,000 IDR. The busses also stops on the way if desired, for example at Probolinggo as a starting point for Bromo-Tengger-Semeru National Park. These busses leave all day, taking an over-night bus in the evening is likely the most convenient.

YOGYAKARTA

Use the air service from Bali on Garuda or AirAsia, with scheduled services early in the morning and late in the evening, making it possible to have a full day of sightseeing in Prambanan and Borobudur and still make it back to your hotel in Bali in time for bed.

BANDUNG

Bandung is near Jakarta, but conveniently serviced from Bali using AirAsia service (flight time around 1+ hour), it is a popular tourist destination for Malaysian visitors and day visitors from Jakarta. Bandung is the centre of garment and textile industry in Indonesia, people go to Bandung looking for bargain clothes and textile in its factory outlets and trade centres. Bandung also famous for its art deco architectural buildings, nice cafes, laid-back lifestyle and cooler air since it is located 700 m above the sea level. It also has some outdoor activities like visits to the nearby semi-active volcano crater and hot spring. Day trips to Bandung are not recommended, better to stay one or two nights in Bandung.

Even as nature robs from below, life continues above and offers a spectacular coastal armchair.

The wonderfully painted traditional watercraft of Bali evoke images of Polynesian outrigger canoes and add an atmosphere of fun to the island's culture.

123

The delights of Bali's high country are never far away, and its natural water features rival the world's best.

SHOPPING

Whether it is simple trinkets, a nice statue or high fashion boutiques that turn you on, Bali is a shopper's paradise. A huge range of very affordable products are offered to the point where shopping can overwhelm a visit if you allow it to!

Fashion

Clothing is a real draw. Popular sportswear brands are available in a multitude of stores in Kuta and Legian for prices approximately thirty to fifty per cent lower than you would pay at home. If the mass market is not your thing, try the ever-increasing number of chic boutiques in Seminyak and support young local designers. Jalan Laksmana is a good starting point.

Arts and Crafts

Bali is an island of artisans, so arts and crafts are always popular. Try to head to the source if you can rather than buying from identikit shops in Kuta or Sanur. You will gain more satisfaction from buying an article direct from the maker and seeing the craftsman in action. Bali has a huge range of locally produced paintings, basketware, stone and wood carvings, silver and shell jewellery, ceramics, natural paper gifts, glassware and much, much more.

Dried Spices and Coffee

These are very popular items to take home. Most supermarkets have specially designed gift packages aimed at tourists, or, if you are visiting Bedugul, buy at the Bukit Mungsu traditional market.

General

Whatever you are buying, make sure you are in your best bargaining mode, as these skills will be required except in the higher-end stores that specifically state that their prices are fixed. And of course, bargaining is a lot of fun. For more general shopping, Bali is home to a myriad of small stores and supermarkets and you will not be short of options. In recent years, 24-hour convenience stores have mushroomed in South Bali with the CircleK and 7/11 franchise chains being especially prominent. The staff at these always speak English, and the product lines they stock are very much aimed at visitors; everything from beer and magazines to western foodstuffs and sun lotion are available around the clock.

EATING AND DRINKING IN BALI

Bali has a huge variety of cafes and restaurants, serving both Indonesian and international food. For better or worse, some American chains have established a presence here, although almost exclusively confined to the southern tourist areas. You will see KFC, McDonald's, Pizza Hut and Starbucks. Interestingly, the menus are often highly adapted to the local tastes. The menu at Pizza Hut looks nothing like one you find in Western countries.

Try the smaller local restaurants rather than touristy ones; the food is better and cheaper. Be sure to try the ubiquitous Indonesian dishes nasi goreng (fried rice), nasi campur (pronounced nasi champur, steamed rice with various vegetables and meats), and mie goreng (fried noodles). These dishes should rarely cost more than Rp 25,000 and are often considerably cheaper.

One of the most delightful experiences to be had in Bali's lies within its mysterious and exciting local markets.

Some of the most authentic food can be found from roving vendors called kaki lima, which literally means five legs. This comprises the three legs of the food cart and the vendor's own two legs. Go to the beaches of Kuta, Legian and Seminyak at sunset and find steaming hot bakso(pronounced ba-so), a delightful meatball and noodle soup, served up fresh for a very inexpensive Rp 5,000. You can season it yourself, but be forewarned - Indonesian spices can be ferociously hot. Go easy until you find your heat tolerance level!

Padang restaurants are a good choice for both the budget-conscious and those visitors wishing to experience authentic Indonesian (but not Balinese) cuisine. These are usually marked with a prominent masakan padang sign and serve food from Padang, Sumatra. The options are usually stacked on plates in the window, you choose what you want and it is served with steamed rice. The most famous Padang speciality is rendang sapi (spicy beef coconut curry) but there are always a number of chicken, fish, egg and vegetable options. Padang food is always halal and you will eat well for Rp 15,000-20,000.

BALINESE CUISINE

Actual Balinese food is common on the island but it has made few inroads in the rest of the country due to its emphasis on pork, which is anathema to the largely Muslim population in the rest of the country. Notable dishes include:

Babi Guling

A roast suckling pig. A large ceremonial dish served with rice that is usually ordered several days in advance, but also often available at night market stalls and selected restaurants. A very notable outlet for babi guling is Ibu Oka's in Ubud. A pilgrimage that needs to be made by many, thanks to Anthony Bourdain, but the numerous stalls around the island also offer an equally delightful experience for half the price of Ibu Oka's.

Bebek Betutu

This is literally darkened duck, topped with a herb paste and roasted in banana leaves over charcoal. The same method can also be used for chicken, resulting in ayam betutu.

Lawar

Covers a range of Balinese salads, usually involving thinly chopped vegetables, minced meat, coconut and spices. Traditionally, blood is mixed into this dish but it is often omitted for the more delicate constitutions of visitors. Green beans and chicken are a particularly common combination.

Sate Lilit

Minced seafood satay, served wrapped around a twig of lemongrass.

Urutan

Balinese spicy sausage, made from pork.

Other local Balinese specialities include:

Ayam Panggang Bumbu Bawang Mentah

Grilled chicken with sliced shallots, chillies and lime.

Ayam Panggang Bumbu Merah

Grilled chicken with red chili and shrimp paste sauce.

Ayam Tutu

Steamed chicken cooked with Balinese herbs and spices.

Tum Ayam/Ketopot

Sliced chicken mixed with herbs and spices and steamed in banana leaves.

Ikan Kakap Bakar Bumbu Terasi

Grilled snapper in local hot spices.

Sudang Lepet

Salted dry fish.

Pepes Ikan Laut

Sliced fish mixed with herbs and spices grilled and served in a banana leaf.

Pelecing Kangkung

Water convolvus with shrimp paste and lime.

Pelecing Paku

Fern tips with shrimp paste and lime

Dietary Restrictions

Unlike Indian Hindus, virtually all Balinese eat meat, and vegetarianism has traditionally been limited to part-time fasts for some priests. It's thus best to assume that all local food is non-vegetarian unless assurances are given to the contrary. In particular, the Indonesian spice paste sambal is a hot paste of ground red chillies, spices and usually shrimp paste. Always check to see if the sambal being served to you contains shrimp paste—you can find it without at a few places. Additionally, kerupuk crackers with a spongy appearance contain shrimp or fish. Instead, ask for emping which is a delicious cracker made from a bean paste and is totally meat free—it resembles a fried potato chip in appearance. However, restaurants catering to tourists do nearly always provide some vegetarian options, and in places like Seminyak and Ubud there are even dedicated vegetarian restaurants.

Halal eateries catering to the Muslim minority exist, but may require a little searching for and tend to be downmarket. Padang restaurants (mentioned above) are a good option. Kosher food is virtually unknown.

Budget

A meal in a basic tourist-oriented restaurant will be around Rp 20,000-50,000/person. In a local restoran or warung the same meal might be about Rp 15,000 or less. Simple warungs sell nasi bungkus (a pyramid shaped paper-wrapped parcel of about 400 g of rice with several tasty extras-to take away) for as little as Rp 3,000-5,000. One very reliable option is nasi campur (rice with several options, chosen by the purchaser) for about Rp 10,000-15,000. Note that rice is often served at ambient temperature with the accompanying food much hotter, this is common practice in Indonesia.

At the other end of the scale, Bali is home to number of truly world-class fine-dining restaurants. Seminyak is home to many of the trendy independent options, and elsewhere on the island, the better five-star resorts have their own very high quality in-house restaurants with prices to match. At all but the cheapest local restaurants, it is normal for 10% government sales tax and 5% service charge to be added to your bill. Some restaurants include this in the price, but most expressly state these plus plus terms.

Everything comes in the most delightfully woven baskets in Bali - from Canang Sari flower baskets to food carriers, shopping baskets or a safe place for the baby.

Drink

The Balinese have nothing against a drink, and alcohol is widely available. However this doesn't mean that drunken behaviour is acceptable.

Indonesia's most popular beer is the ubiquitous Bintang, but the cheaper Bali Hai is nearly as widespread. Bintang is a fairly highly regarded classic light Asian beer, Bali Hai is a lager, and despite the name it's actually brewed in a suburb of Jakarta. The Bali-based microbrew Storm is available in several different flavors, and the pale ale is especially good. The Storm beer is more expensive though. The other local beer is Anker. Both Carlsberg and San Miguel are brewed locally under license. A wide range of more expensive imported beers are also available. Beer is relatively expensive in local terms, though still cheap by western standards; at Rp 15,000 and up a small bottle costs the same as a full meal in a local eatery. In tourist centres, happy hours are widely publicised before and after sunset, with regular (stubbie) bottles of beer going for Rp 10,000 to 20,000 and the large bottles for Rp 18,000 to 30,000.

Bali produces its own wines, with Hatten being the oldest and most popular brand, available in white, red, rose (most popular) and sparkling varieties. Quality is inconsistent, but the rose is usually OK and much cheaper than imported wines, which can easily top Rp 300,000 per bottle. Wine aficionados are better off bringing their own bottle in with them. Most restaurants will let you bring your own bottle and some will charge a modest corkage fee. Smaller establishments may not have a corkscrew, so bring your own!

Bali also produces its own liqueurs and spirits, with Bali Moon being the most popular. They offer a wide range of flavoured liqueurs: banana, blackcurrant, butterscotch, coconut, hazelnut, lychee, melon, peppermint, orange, blue curaçao, pineapple and coffee. Vodka and other spirits are also produced locally, with Mansion House being the most popular brand. Be aware, though, that many of these local spirits are little more than flavoured rice liquor. Cocktails in Bali range from Rp 30,000 in small bars to Rp 100,000 in high end establishments. Bali Moon cocktails are available in almost every bar, restaurant and hotel in Bali. Liqueurs are available in many retail outlets; just enquire within if you wish to have fun making your own cocktails!

Bali's traditional hooches are arak, a clear distilled spirit that packs a 40° punch; brem, a fermented rice wine sold in gift shops in attractive clay bottles that are much nicer than the taste of the stuff inside; and tuak, a palm wine that is often served at traditional festivities. Visitors should be extremely careful about where they purchase arak, as there have been a number of serious poisoning cases and even some deaths involving tainted arak.

Tap water in Bali is not drinkable, but bottled water is universally available and extremely inexpensive (Rp 5,000 or so for a 1.5 litre bottle); restaurants usually use commercially purified water for cooking. The most popular brand is Aqua and that name is often used generically for bottled water. Filtered water shops are also common, providing on-site treatment of the mains water to a potable standard. This is known as air putih (literally white water). These shops are much cheaper than retail outlets, selling water for about Rp 5,000 per 11-litre reusable container, and they avoid the waste created by plastic bottles.

Very cheap (about Rp 15,000) are fresh fruit juices and their mixes (it can be watermelon, melon, papaya, orange, lime, banana or almost any other fruit you can think of). In Bali, avocado (alpukat) is used as a dessert fruit. Blended with sugar, a little water and ice—and sometimes chocolate syrup—this is a beverage you will rarely find elsewhere! If you do not drink alcohol, Bali's fresh juices in various creative combinations will please you no end. Almost all restaurant menus have a section devoted to various non-alcoholic fruit-based drinks.

Fresh, authentic and the backbone of Balinese cuisine - the island's herbs and spices bring an exotic feel to any dish.

144

Fresh food is the key to enjoying the best of Bali's local produce.

Straight from the sea to the plate - is there any other way to eat seafood?

One of the most striking things about food in Bali is its outwardly simple appearance.
Simplicity in the serving understates the delicate blend of spices that turn the ordinary into the
extraordinary.

ACCOMMODATION

Bali has, without a doubt, the best range of accommodation in Indonesia, from Rp60,000 per night ($6) losmens to US$4,000 per night super-homes.

The backpackers tend to head for Kuta, which has the cheapest digs on the island. However, if the accommodation is located near a night club they can be noisy at night. One quiet and clean place in the cheaper category is Hotel Oka in Jalan Padma in Legian, only a kilometre from the night clubs of Kuta and walking distance from the beach.

Many of the numerous five-star resorts are clustered in Nusa Dua, Seminyak and Ubud. Sanur and Jimbaran offer a fairly happy compromise if you want beaches and some quiet. Ubud's hotels and resorts cater to those who prefer spas and cultural pursuits over surfing and booze. Legian is situated between Kuta and Seminyak and offers a good range of accommodation. The newest area to start offering a wide range of accommodation is Uluwatu which now boasts everything from surfer bungalows to the opulent Bulgari Hotel. Further north on the west coast is the district of Canggu, which offers many traditional villages set among undulating rice fields and a good range of accommodation. For rest and revitalisation, visit Amed, an area of peaceful fishing villages on the east coast with some good hotels and restaurants, or head for the sparsely populated areas of West Bali.

Thanks to Bali's balmy climate, many hotels, bungalows and villas offer open-air bathrooms, often set in a lush garden. They look amazing and are definitely a very Balinese experience, but they may also shelter little uninvited guests and are best avoided if you have a low tolerance for critters. Bali hotel prices may be given in three different currencies. Prices in U.S. dollars are most common, particularly away from the budget sector. Euros are sometimes used, particularly at hotels owned by European nationals. Lower-end places usually (but not always) price in Indonesian Rupiah. If you pay your bill by credit card, then the amount in the currency you agreed to when making the booking is converted to Indonesian Rupiah on the day you pay and your account is charged with that amount of Rupiah. This is because Indonesian banking law does not permit credit card transactions in any other currency. If you pay by cash, you can settle with the currency in which you were quoted the room rate.

It is important to understand the tax and service charge that hotels are obliged to levy by Indonesian law. All high-end and mid-range (and a fair proportion of budget) hotels will levy a 21% tax and service charge on the room rate (the so-called "plus plus"). When you make a booking, you should always ask whether the rate quoted includes or excludes this. Simple budget homestays/losmen and informal accommodation are not obliged to levy these charges. The 21% consists of 11% sales tax which goes to the government and a 10% service charge which goes into a pool shared between the staff.

Every type of getaway can be found in Bali - including those that offer accommodation and service that is among the world's finest.

Private Villas

Bali has become famous for its large collection of private villas for rent, complete with staff and top-class levels of service. Low labour costs result in single villas boasting staff teams of up to 30 people at the really high end. A private villa rental can be a great option for a visit to Bali, but it pays to be aware of the potential pitfalls. Not every place sold as a villa actually fits the bill. Prices vary widely and some operators claim to go as low as US$30 per night (which usually means a standalone bungalow on hotel grounds with little actual privacy). Realistically, you will be looking at upwards of US$200 per night for anything with a decent location and a private pool. At the top of the range, nightly rents can easily go north of US$1,000. The general rule of you get what you pay for applies here. There are, of course, exceptions, but a 4 bedroom villa offered for US$400 and one for US$800 per night will be different in many ways—the standard of maintenance, the number of staff and their English ability, and the overall quality of furnishings and fittings in the property.

Look carefully as to who is running the villa. Is it run by the owner, a local company, a Western company or by local staff who answer to an absent overseas owner? And who you are renting through - directly from the owner, a management company, an established villa agent or one who just opened a month ago after his friend Nyoman told him how easy it was? Each path has its pros and cons. If it is an agency, see if there are press reviews. Ask how long the villa has been taking commercial guests, as villas normally take a year or so to get to best service levels. In the first six to 12 months of operation, great villas may offer introductory rates that are well below market value to gain awareness. In all circumstances thoroughly examine and query the security arrangements, especially if dealing with an apparently inexperienced or opportunistic operator to ensure you are not exposing yourself or your belongings to any unnecessary risks.

Private villas are found mostly in the greater Seminyak area (Seminyak, Umalas, Canggu), in the south around Jimbaran and Uluwatu, in Sanur and around the hill town of Ubud as well as Lovina in north Bali . They are rare in heavily built-up areas like Kuta, Legian and Denpasar.

Long-Term Accommodations

For an extended stay, it is worth considering a long-term rental, which can be as low as US$4,000 per year. Restaurants, shops and bars frequented by Bali's sizable expatriate community, particularly in Seminyak, Sanur and Ubud, are good places to find information about long-term rentals. Look for a bulletin board with property advertisements tacked up or pick up a copy of the local expat biweekly publication, The Bali Advertiser. Remember that with a year-round tourism trade, villas that have everything right are usually available for more lucrative short-term rental only. Long-term rental houses tend to be older and not as well maintained. If you are willing to be flexible, though, you can find nice house options over a wide range of budgets.

Often, Bali's beaches and tropical forests are depicted in tourism material, but it also has a magnificent coastline that features stunning cliffs and caves.

Only society's fortunate few could afford such a place in the past, but Bali now offers the height of luxury to people like you and me.

There is an incredible stillness to be found in some parts of in Bali, and it often lies only a heartbeat away.

The relationship between nature and interior design combines beautifully to create a tropical haven in the most stunning of settings.

161

Bali is notorious for its ability to deliver an instant change of pace around every corner. From packed beaches to hidden waterfalls, mountain getaways, white water rafting and island hopping, there are many more surprising sights and experiences to be found around the next bend.

Even poolside, attention to detail is part of the Balinese tourist's experience.

STAYING SAFE IN BALI

Bali is, in general, a safe destination, and few visitors encounter any real problems.

Bali was the scene of lethal terrorist bombings in 2002 and 2005, with both waves of attacks targeting nightclubs and restaurants popular among foreign visitors. Security is consequently tight at obvious targets, but it is of course impossible to protect oneself fully against terrorism. If it is any reassurance, the Balinese themselves—who depend on tourism for their livelihood—deplored the bombings and the terrorists behind them for the terrible suffering they have caused on this peaceful island. As a visitor, it is important to put the risk in perspective: the sad fact is that Bali's roads are, statistically, far more dangerous than even the deadliest bomb. It may still be prudent to avoid high-profile western hang-outs, especially those without security measures. The paranoid or just security-conscious may wish to head out of the tourist enclaves of South Bali to elsewhere on the island.

Drugs

Bali is increasingly enforcing Indonesia's harsh penalties against the import, export, trafficking and possession of illegal drugs, including marijuana, ecstasy, cocaine and heroin. Several high profile arrests of foreigners have taken place in Bali since 2004, and a number have been sentenced to lengthy prison terms or (very rarely) execution. Even the possession of a small amount of drugs for personal use puts you at risk of a trial and prison sentence. Watch out for seemingly harmless street boys looking to sell you drugs (marijuana, ecstasy, cocaine, etc.). More often than not, they are working with undercover police **and will try to sell you** drugs so that they can then get uniformed officers onto you. The police officers will (if you are lucky) demand a bribe for your release, or, more likely, look for a far larger payday by taking you into custody. Just avoid Bali's drug scene at all costs. The unfortunate people who are caught and processed will find there is little distinction between personal use and dealing in the eyes of the Indonesian legal system. 'Expedition fees', monies paid to shorten jail or prison time, can easily run to US$20,000 and are often a lot more.

There is a fair chance that you will be offered magic mushrooms, especially if you are young and find yourself in Kuta. Indonesian law is a little unclear in this area but with the whole country in the midst of a drug crackdown since 2004, it is not worth taking the risk.

Water Safety

If you see a red flag planted in the sand, do not swim there, as they are a warning of dangerous rip currents. These currents can pull you out to sea with alarming speed and even the strongest swimmers cannot swim against them. The thing to do is to stay calm and swim sideways (along the shore) until out of the rip and only then head for the shore. The ocean is not to be trifled with in Bali, and dozens of people, some experienced some not, die by drowning every year.

Bali's beaches offer virtually everything the waterside can give - snorkelling, pleasure cruises and island hopping are but a few of those experiences.

Scams

Petty scams are not uncommon, although they can usually be avoided with a modicum of common sense. If approached on the street by anybody offering a deal on souvenirs, transport, etc., you can rest assured that you will pay more if you follow your new found friend. Guard your bags, especially at transport terminals and ferry terminals. In addition to the risk of them being stolen, self-appointed porters like to grab them without warning and then insist on ridiculous prices for their services.

Timeshare scams are common in Bali with several high profile, apparently legitimate operators. If you are approached by a very friendly street canvasser asking you to complete a survey and then attend a holiday resort presentation to claim your prize (this is inevitably a free holiday, which you end up paying for anyway), politely refuse and walk away. You may also be cold-called at your hotel to be told you have 'won a holiday' - the caller may even know your name and nationality thanks to a tip-off from someone who has already seen your data. If you fall for this scam, you will be subjected to a very long, high-pressure sales presentation and if you actually buy the 'holiday club' product, you will certainly regret it. Timeshare is a completely unregulated industry in Indonesia, and you have no recourse.

When leaving Bali, if you have anything glass in your baggage (such as duty-free alcohol) the security guards may put some pressure on you to have it wrapped to keep it safe, and it can seem like it's a requirement rather than a suggestion (it is Rp 60,000 a bag). Similarly, when arriving in Bali, some airport officials may offer to take your bags for you and walk you through customs, be generally friendly and helpful, and then demand a tip.

Money Changing

The money changing rule is simple: use only authorised money changers with proper offices and always ask for a receipt. The largest is called PT Central Kuta and they have several outlets. If you are especially nervous, then use a formal bank. You may get a better rate at an authorised money changer though.

Avoid changing money in smaller currency exchange offices located within shops, as they more often than not will try to steal money by using very creative and "magician"-like methods. Often the rate advertised on the street is nowhere near the rate that they will give you in the end. Many times the rate is set higher to lure you in so that they can con you out of a banknote or two, and when this is not possible, they will give you a shoddy rate and state that the difference is due to commission. This even applies to the places which clearly state that there is no commission. If you do get your money changed, always be the last person to count and touch it before you leave the shop. Do not rely on the money changer to count it even if they do it in front of you.

Hawkers and Peddlers

For many, the largest irritant will be the hawkers and peddlers who linger around temples, malls, beaches, and anywhere tourists congregate. It may feel difficult or rude to ignore the constant come-ons to buy souvenirs, food, and assorted junk, but it can be necessary in order to enjoy your holiday in semi-peace.

Monkeys

Last but not least be wary around the monkeys that occupy many temples (most notably Uluwatu and Ubud's Monkey Forest). They are experts at stealing

Many come for the nightlife, others stumble upon the excitement of what the night has to offer, while others have yet to discover the upbeat side of Bali.

possessions like glasses, cameras and even handbags, and have been known to attack people carrying food. Feeding them is just asking for trouble.

Rabies is present in Bali, and several deaths arising from rabies infections have been recorded. Visitors to the island should avoid contact with dogs, cats, monkeys and other animals that carry the disease. If bitten, seek medical attention.

Staying Healthy When in Bali

Although the standards of healthcare and emergency facilities have improved greatly in recent years, they remain below what most visitors would be accustomed to in their home country. Whilst minor illness and injury can be adequately treated in the ubiquitous local clinics most overseas visitors would not be comfortable having serious problems dealt with in a local hospital, and insurance coverage for emergency medical evacuation is therefore a wise precaution. If a medical evacuation is required, patients are normally moved to Singapore or Perth. Jakarta, Indonesia's capital, does however have some high standard medical care facilities if seeking medical attention at a closer location.

Be aware that the purchase of travel insurance still means that most clinics and hospitals may require payment in advance, or sometimes by incremental payment as various services are rendered. This may require access to a quite significant amount of cash to keep things moving. Any claim is then made to the insurance company upon your return home. This is almost always the case if the problem is one that can be dealt with on an outpatient basis. Make sure that your insurance company has an agreement with the provider or immediately establishes one, otherwise you will also be landed with a bill for an inpatient stay. Bali

International Medical Centre (BIMC) has agreements with many insurance companies and is a well serviced hospital. This is however a relatively expensive option and even they ask for payment for outpatient treatments.

The major travel insurance companies may be slow to respond with appropriate assistance and equally slow to refer a claimant to a suitable medical service. Delays may also be experienced if the insurer is slow or indecisive in authorising treatment. Difficulties may arise from an insurer not authorising a payment guarantee to the local medical services provider. Delays in rendering appropriate treatment are a common outcome. Try to gain an understanding of the policy terms and limitations of your travel insurance cover prior to departing your home country. Trying to gain an understanding of the limitations of cover whilst amidst a crisis is not recommended. Some insurance companies and their emergency response centres may not live up to your own expectations of regional knowledge, appropriate case management and speedy response. Your best insurance is always common-sense, some basic pre-departure research on your destination and the application of good situational awareness whilst travelling. Try to have your own plan in place to deal with any crisis you may encounter when travelling rather than relying solely upon a possibly inadequately skilled and under-qualified person sitting in a distant call centre who may have their own role complicated by problems with language, communication and access to the insurers decision makers. You may wish to consider carrying the names and contact numbers of one or two of the major local medical and evacuation providers in your wallet or purse so that you know how to quickly obtain medical assistance should an emergency arise. Always ensure that you contact your

Visit Ubud and its monkey sanctuary and you'll never look at our Simian cousins the same again. Noisy, mischievous and utterly fascinating, they are part of what makes Ubud so unique.

insurer as soon as possible should an emergency arise otherwise you may find they are later unwilling to accept liability for payment for any expenses that arise. Always keep a thorough record of all expenditures and communications with your insurer and obtain full and detailed invoices and receipts for all services provided and any incidental costs. If you do not understand the detail of anything that you are billed for ask for an explanation; if information is not forthcoming withhold payment or authorisation until such time as an acceptable explanation is given.

International SOS Indonesia (AEA SOS Medika) was founded in Indonesia in 1984 and has grown into an international organisation handling around 9 million cases per year. It has a professionally staffed and operated clinic in Bali. They offer clinic services, hospital referral and emergency medical evacuation services. They have agreements or associations in place with many of the major travel insurers and are a principal medical service supplier in the SE Asian region, including Indonesia.

Protection From the Sun

The midday sun in Bali will fry the unwary traveller to a crisp, so slap on plenty of high-factor sun-protection and drink lots of fluids. However there is no need to carry litres of water as you can buy a bottle virtually anywhere. The locals tend to stay away from the beaches until about two hours before sunset, when most of the ferocity has gone out of the sun.

Safety While Surfing

Surfers often experience coral cuts or more serious injuries on the sharp reefs, so it is highly recommended to get Travel Insurance with full Emergency Med-Evac cover. Indo Surf Travel Insurance is now available, which

is the only company to cover damage to surfboards even while in use surfing.

Nasties

Travelling to Bali may expose you to some risks in contracting one of many tropical diseases that are present in the region. Bali is officially a malaria-free zone, but dengue fever is a problem and all sensible precautions should be taken against being bitten by mosquitoes.

Take care in restaurants and bars; although it is very rare nowadays, some may use untreated/unsafe tap water to make ice for drinks otherwise made with clean ingredients. Tap water in hotels should not be used for drinking or brushing teeth unless explicitly labelled as safe.

Both drink adulteration with methyl alcohol (methanol) and drink spiking in bars and clubs is not uncommon in Bali. Sensible precautions should be taken when buying and consuming beverages. From 2009 until now (2012) a number of Indonesians and visiting tourists in Java, Bali and Lombok/Gilli Islands have been poisoned by consuming drinks containing methyl alcohol resulting in fatalities. Methyl alcohol (wood alcohol) and other contaminants are highly dangerous and have been found in some locally produced alcoholic drinks including locally made Arak although precautions must also be taken when buying any mixed drink. The initial symptoms of methyl alcohol/**methanol intoxication** include central nervous system depression, headache, dizziness, nausea, lack of co-ordination and confusion. If methyl alcohol poisoning is suspected, seek medical assistance immediately.

The HIV infection rate in Bali is increasing, mainly amongst sex workers of both genders and intravenous drug users. If you engage in any risky activity, always protect yourself.

EMERGENCY CONTACT NUMBERS IN BALI

BY PHONE

Ambulance
118

Indonesian Red Cross (PMI) & free ambulance service.
(+62) 361 480282

Police
110

Search & Rescue Team
115 or 151, (+62) 361 751111

Tourist Police
(+62) 361 754599 or (+62) 361 763753

Bali Police HQ
Jl WR Supratman, Denpasar
(+62) 361 227711

Badung Police HQ
Jl Gunung Sanghyang, Denpasar
(+62) 361 424245

POLICE STATIONS

Denpasar
Jl Ahmad Yani
(+62) 361 225456
Sanur
Jl By Pass Ngurah Rai
(+62) 361 288597

Kuta
Jl Raya Tuban
(+62) 361 751598
Nusa Dua
Jl By Pass Nusa Dua
(+62) 361 772110

HOSPITALS WITH 24 HOURS EMERGENCY ROOM (ER)

RS Umum Sanglah
Jl Kesehatan 1, Denpasar
(+62) 361 243307, 227911, 225483, 265064.

RS Umum Badung
Jl Raya Kapal Mengwi, Denpasar
(+62) 361 7421880.

RS Umum Dharma Usadha
Jl Jend Sudirman 50, Denpasar
(+62) 361 227560, 233786, 233787.

RS Umum Manuaba
Jl HOS Cokroaminoto 28, Denpasar
(+62) 361 426393, 226393.

RS Umum Surya Husadha
Jl Pulau Serangan 1-3, Denpasar
(+62) 361 233787

RS Umum Wangaya
Jl RA Kartini 133, Denpasar
(+62) 361 222141

PHONES IN BALI

Unfortunately, it is very unlikely you will find a working public telephone on the street, which can be very frustrating in emergency situations. Today, most tourists merely ensure that their carrier can enable them to continue using their normal mobile phone when overseas. For others, they may have to rely on locally sourced mobile phones (local SIM cards may be used in unlocked phones with economical local and international calling rates) or phone/internet shops. Purchasing a local SIM card is recommended if you foresee that you will have to make multiple calls during your stay. There are several cellular operators In Bali: Telkomsel (simPATI) and Indosat (IM3) have the largest coverage area. In addition to the GSM standard, you can find CDMA (operator Smart).

Local calls from hotel rooms are charged an expensive flagfall and per minute rate. Budget accommodation options are unlikely to offer telephone services to guests.

AREA CODES

Bali has six area codes.

0361

All of South Bali (Bukit Peninsula, Canggu, Denpasar, Jimbaran, Legian, Nusa Dua, Sanur, Seminyak, Tanah Lot) plus Gianyar, Tabanan and Ubud)

0362

Lovina, Pemuteran and Singaraja

0363

Amed, Candidasa, Karangasem, Kintamani, Padang Bai, Tirta Gangga

0365

Negara, Gilimanuk, Medewi Beach, West Bali National Park

0366

Bangli, Besakih, Kintamani, Klungkung, Mount Agung, Nusa Ceningan, Nusa Lembongan, Nusa Penida

0368

Bedugul

The depth and ancient spiritualism of Bali's traditional dances originate from as far away as India, and similarities in costumes and their accessories sometimes hint at ancient battles between good and evil.

INTERNET

Airport Wifi

The airport has free wifi under Telkom's @wifi.id program, accessible from most passenger areas in both terminals. The access point is usually named @ NgurahRaiAirport. Upon connecting, it should present a popup window with an often-hidden orange connect button - if you can't find it, it may be clipped to the right side of the screen. A confirmation page with advertisements will follow, which can be safely closed. This provides reasonably fast (by Indonesian standards) internet, good enough for a video call and moderate browsing. It's not clear if this wifi has any sort of time or quota limitation.

Keep in mind that this is a public and unsecured wifi, so be absolutely sure that any private browsing is encrypted or simply play it safe and avoid sensitive activity. Lounges may offer their own, encrypted wifi networks

ELECTRICAL CONNECTIONS

Electricity is supplied at 220V 50Hz. Outlets are the European standard CEE-7/7 Schukostecker or Schuko or the compatible, but non-grounded, CEE-7/16 Europlug types. American and Canadian travellers should pack a voltage-changing adapter for these outlets if they plan to use North American electrical equipment (although a lot of electronics with power adapters will work on 220 volts, check your equipment first).